D0596659

Hope is a renewable option: if you run out of it at the end of the day, you get to start over in the morning. —*Barbara Kingsolver*

Everything that is done in the

world *is done by hope.*

—*Dr. Martin Luther King Jr.*

{ QUOTES ON }

HOPE *and* VIRTUE

edited by Suzanne Gibbs Taylor

GIBBS SMITH
TO ENRICH AND INSPIRE HUMANKIND
Salt Lake City | Charleston | Santa Fe | Santa Barbara

First Edition
13 12 11 10 09   5 4 3 2 1

Text © 2009 Gibbs Smith
Quote on front cover from Thomas Paine, as quoted
in the inaugural address of Barack Obama.

Published by
Gibbs Smith
P.O. Box 667
Layton, Utah 84041

1.800.835.4993 orders
www.gibbs-smith.com

Designed by Black Eye Design
Printed and bound in the United States of America
Gibbs Smith books are printed on either recycled,
100% post-consumer waste, FSC-certified papers
or on paper produced from a 100% certified
sustainable forest/controlled wood source.

Library of Congress Control Number: 2009925655
ISBN 13: 978-1-4236-0674-1
ISBN 10: 1-4236-0674-4

OUR CHALLENGES MAY BE NEW. THE INSTRUMENTS WITH WHICH WE MEET THEM MAY BE NEW. BUT THOSE VALUES UPON WHICH OUR SUCCESS DEPENDS—honesty and hard work, courage and fair play, tolerance and curiosity, loyalty and patriotism—these things are old. THESE THINGS ARE TRUE. THEY HAVE BEEN THE QUIET FORCE OF PROGRESS THROUGHOUT HISTORY. *—Barack Obama*

★ ★ ★

The natural flights of the human mind are not from pleasure to pleasure but FROM HOPE TO HOPE. —*Samuel Johnson*

★ ★ ★ ————————

The important thing
is not that we can
live on hope alone,
BUT THAT LIFE IS
NOT WORTH LIVING
WITHOUT IT. —*Harvey Milk*

All human wisdom
is summed up in two
words—WAIT AND
HOPE. —*Alexander Dumas*

Hope is the thing with feathers, that perches in the soul, and sings the tune without words, and never stops at all. *—Emily Dickinson*

I always

entertain great hopes. —*Robert Frost*

★ ★ ★

HOPE SPRINGS ETERNAL

in the human breast.

—*Alexander Pope*

Hope

has as many lives as a cat or a king. —*Henry Wadsworth Longfellow*

THE CAPACITY FOR HOPE is the most significant fact of life. It provides human beings with a sense of destination and the energy to get started. —*Norman Cousins*

★ ★ ★

Hope is the companion of power, and the mother of success; *for who so hopes strongly* has within him the gift of miracles. —*Samuel Smiles*

——— ★ ★ ★ ———

HOPE is the last thing
ever lost. —*Italian Proverb*

CONSULT NOT YOUR FEARS BUT YOUR hopes and dreams. THINK NOT ABOUT YOUR FRUSTRATIONS, BUT ABOUT YOUR UNFULFILLED POTENTIAL. CONCERN YOURSELF NOT WITH WHAT YOU TRIED AND FAILED IN, BUT WITH WHAT IS STILL POSSIBLE FOR YOU TO DO. *—Pope John XXIII*

HOPE IS putting faith

to work when doubting would

be easier. —*Unknown*

★ ★ ★

Great
hopes

make great men. —*Thomas Fuller*

★ ★ ★

He who does not HOPE
TO WIN has already
lost. —*José Joaquin Olmedo*

Through humor, you can soften some of the worst blows that life delivers. And once you find laughter, no matter how painful your situation might be, you can survive it. —*Bill Cosby*

MANY OF THE GREAT ACHIEVEMENTS OF

THE WORLD WERE ACCOMPLISHED BY TIRED

AND DISCOURAGED MEN AND WOMEN

who kept on working. —*Unknown*

WE ARE ALL IN THE
GUTTER, but some of us are
looking at the stars. —*Oscar Wilde*

★ ★ ★

Hope never

abandons you; you abandon it.

—*George Weinberg*

★ ★ ★

Learn from yesterday, live for today,

hope for tomorrow.

—*Albert Einstein*

IN ALL THINGS it is

better to hope than to despair.

—*Johann Wolfgang von Goethe*

Hope

is the dream of a soul awake. —*French Proverb*

What seems to us as
bitter trials are often
BLESSINGS IN DISGUISE.

—*Oscar Wilde*

★ ★ ★

Hope
is faith

holding out its hand in
the dark. —*George Iles*

Dum spiro spero:

*"While I breathe,
I hope."* —*Latin Proverb*

ONE VOICE can change a room, and if one voice can change a room, then it can change a city, and if it can change a city, it can change a state, and if it can change a state, it can change a nation, and if it can change a nation, it can change the world. Your voice can change the world. —*Barack Obama*

MOST OF THE IMPORTANT THINGS IN
THE WORLD HAVE BEEN ACCOMPLISHED
BY PEOPLE who have kept on
trying WHEN THERE SEEMED TO BE
NO HOPE AT ALL. —*Dale Carnegie*

★ ★ ★

WHAT WOULD LIFE BE

if we had no courage

to attempt anything?

—*Vincent van Gogh*

Hope is important

because it can make the present moment

less difficult to bear. If we believe that

tomorrow will be better, we can bear a

hardship today. —*Thich Nhat Hanh*

He who has health, has hope.
And he who has hope, has
everything.

—Proverb

Wisdom is knowing WHAT TO DO NEXT, SKILL IS KNOWING HOW TO DO IT, AND VIRTUE IS DOING IT. —*David Starr Jordan*

Courage

is not simply one of the virtues,
but the form of every virtue at the
testing point. —*C. S. Lewis*

We do not place especial value on the

possession of a virtue

until we notice its total absence in

our opponent. —*Friedrich Nietzsche*

★ ★ ★

THE SUPERIOR MAN
THINKS ALWAYS OF
VIRTUE; the common
man thinks of
comfort. —*Confucius*

Virtue is reason

which has become energy.

—*Karl Wilhelm Friedrich Schlegel*

JUST AS TREASURES

are uncovered from the earth, so
virtue appears from good deeds,
and wisdom appears from a pure
and peaceful mind. To walk safely
through the maze of human life,
one needs the light of wisdom and
the guidance of virtue. —*Buddha*

★ ★ ★

Happiness

is neither virtue nor pleasure
nor this thing nor that
but simply growth. We
are happy when we are
growing. —*William Butler Yeats*

★ ★ ★

WHO SOWS VIRTUE reaps

honor. —*Leonardo da Vinci*

Hope

is the only bee that

makes honey without

flowers. —*Robert Ingersoll*

COURAGE IS THE MOST important of all the virtues, because without courage, you can't practice any other virtue consistently. You can practice any virtue erratically, but nothing consistently without courage. —*Maya Angelou*

Beauty virtue without is like a

rose without scent. —*Proverb*

All virtue

is summed up in dealing justly. —*Aristotle*

★ ★ ★

GLORY FOLLOWS

VIRTUE as if it were

its shadow. —*Cicero*

The power of a man's

virtue should not be measured

by his special efforts, but by his

ordinary doing. —*Blaise Pascal*

★ ★ ★

Some rise by sin, and some by virtue fall. —*William Shakespeare*

In all pleasure

hope is a considerable part.

—*Samuel Johnson*

Always do the right thing.

THIS WILL GRATIFY SOME PEOPLE AND

ASTONISH THE REST. —*Mark Twain*

Virtue is virtue only when it is spontaneous; virtue is virtue only when it is natural, unpracticed—WHEN IT COMES OUT OF YOUR VISION, OUT OF YOUR AWARENESS, OUT OF YOUR UNDERSTANDING.

—*Bhagwan Shree Rajneesh*

So shines

a good deed in a weary world. —*Willy Wonka*

★ ★ ★

It has been my experience
that FOLKS WHO HAVE
NO VICES have very few
virtues. —*Abraham Lincoln*

Sincerity and truth

are the basis of every virtue. —*Confucius*

WISDOM IS KNOWING

what to do next; virtue is doing it.

—*David Starr Jordan*

To practice five things under all circumstances constitutes perfect virtue; THESE FIVE ARE GRAVITY, GENEROSITY OF SOUL, SINCERITY, EARNESTNESS, AND KINDNESS. —*Confucius*

★ ★ ★

Let us be true: this is the highest

maxim of art and of life, the secret of
eloquence and of virtue, and of all moral
authority. —*Henri Frederic Amiel*

Faith is the sense

of life, that sense by virtue of which

man does not destroy himself, but

continues to live on. It is the force

whereby we live. —*Leo Tolstoy*

Kindness

is the sunshine in which virtue grows. —*Robert Green*

TO DESIRE AND STRIVE

to be of some service to the world,

to aim at doing something which

shall really increase the happiness and

welfare and virtue of mankind—THIS

IS A CHOICE WHICH IS POSSIBLE FOR

ALL OF US; AND SURELY IT IS A GOOD

HAVEN TO SAIL FOR. —*Henry van Dyke*

★ ★ ★

He who has health,
has hope; and HE
WHO HAS HOPE, has
everything. —*Thomas Carlyle*

★ ★ ★

Hope will

never be silent. *—Harvey Milk*

Where there is *no vision,*

there is *no hope.*

—*George Washington Carver*

The
mind is never satisfied
with the objects immediately before
it, but is always breaking away from
the present moment, and losing itself
in schemes of future felicity . . . The
natural flights of the human mind
are not from pleasure to pleasure, but
from hope to hope. —*Samuel Johnson*

What is true OF THE INDIVIDUAL
WILL BE TOMORROW TRUE OF THE
WHOLE NATION IF INDIVIDUALS
WILL BUT REFUSE TO LOSE HEART
AND HOPE. —*Mahatma Gandhi*

HOPE CHANGES
EVERYTHING, doesn't it?

—*Diane Sawyer*

★ ★ ★

HOPE IS THE WORD
which God has written
on the brow of every
man. —*Victor Hugo*

Optimism is the faith

that leads to achievement. Nothing

can be done without hope and

confidence. *—Helen Keller*

Three grand essentials to happiness IN THIS LIFE ARE SOMETHING TO DO, SOMETHING TO LOVE, AND SOMETHING TO HOPE FOR. —*Joseph Addison*

I believe that imagination is stronger than knowledge. That myth is more potent than history. That dreams are more powerful than facts. That hope always triumphs over experience. That laughter is the only cure for grief. And I believe that love is stronger than death. —*Robert Fulghum*

There is no medicine like hope, NO INCENTIVE SO GREAT, AND NO TONIC SO POWERFUL AS EXPECTATION OF SOMETHING TOMORROW. —*Orison Swett Marden*

IF CHILDREN have the ability to ignore all odds and percentages, then maybe we can all learn from them. When you think about it, what other choice is there but to hope? We have two options, medically and emotionally: give up or Fight Like Hell. —*Lance Armstrong*

Just as despair can come to one only

from other human beings, hope, too,

can be *given to one* only by

other human beings. —*Elie Wiesel*

THE GREATEST JOYS ARE found not only in what we do and feel, but also in what we hope for. —*Bryant H. McGill*

If you wish to succeed in life, make perseverance your bosom friend, experience your wise counselor, caution your elder brother, and hope your guardian genius. —*Joseph Addison*

★ ★ ★

Hope is some
extraordinary spiritual
GRACE that GOD GIVES US
to control our fears,
not to oust them.

—*Vincent McNabb*

HOPE BEGINS in the dark,

the stubborn hope that if you just

show up and try to do the right thing,

the dawn will come. —*Anne Lamott*

THE BEST WAY NOT TO FEEL HOPELESS is to get up and do something. DON'T WAIT FOR GOOD THINGS TO HAPPEN TO YOU. IF YOU GO OUT AND MAKE SOME GOOD THINGS HAPPEN, YOU WILL FILL THE WORLD WITH HOPE, YOU WILL FILL YOURSELF WITH HOPE. —*Barack Obama*

Hope, THAT STAR OF

LIFE'S TREMULOUS

OCEAN. —*Paul Moon James*

Virtue is the fount whence

honor springs. —*Christopher Marlowe*

Sweet ARE THE SLUMBERS OF THE VIRTUOUS MAN. —*Joseph Addison*

In the approach to virtue, there are

many steps. —*Cicero*

BETTER KEEP yourself
clean and bright. You are the window
through which you must see the
world. —*George Bernard Shaw*

Think no vice so small that you may commit it, and no virtue so small that you may overlook it. —*Confucius*

★ ★ ★

VIRTUE CONSISTS, not
in abstaining from vice,
but in not desiring it.

—*George Bernard Shaw*

★ ★ ★

There is no road or ready way to

virtue.

—*Sir Thomas Browne*

Hope is a state of mind, NOT OF THE WORLD. HOPE, IN THIS DEEP AND POWERFUL SENSE, IS NOT THE SAME AS JOY THAT THINGS ARE GOING WELL, OR WILLINGNESS TO INVEST IN ENTERPRISES THAT ARE OBVIOUSLY HEADING FOR SUCCESS, BUT RATHER AN ABILITY TO WORK FOR SOMETHING BECAUSE IT IS GOOD. —*Vaclav Havel*

★ ★ ★

MAY EVERY SUNRISE

hold more promise,

every moonrise hold

more peace. —*Anonymous*

Aerodynamically, the bumblebee shouldn't be able to fly, but the bumblebee doesn't know it so it goes on flying anyway. —*Mary Kay Ash*

HOPE, like the gleaming taper's light,

ADORNS and cheers our way;

AND still, as darker grows the night,

EMITS a brighter ray.

—Oliver Goldsmith

THE HOME IS THE CHIEF

school of human virtue.

—*William Ellery Channing*

Virtue is

a state of war, and to live in it
we have always to combat with
ourselves. —*Jean Jacques Rousseau*

Let your hook be

always cast. In the pool where you least expect it, will be fish. —*Ovid*

The present is the ever moving shadow

that divides yesterday from tomorrow.

In that lies hope.

—*Frank Lloyd Wright*

The mark of your ignorance IS THE DEPTH OF YOUR BELIEF IN INJUSTICE AND TRAGEDY. WHAT THE CATERPILLAR CALLS THE END OF THE WORLD, THE MASTER CALLS A BUTTERFLY. —*Anonymous*

LET'S HAVE FAITH

that right makes might; and in that faith
let us, to the end, dare to do our duty as
we understand it. —*Abraham Lincoln*

GREAT NECESSITIES CALL

out great virtues.

—*Abigail Adams*

Men are equal;

it is not birth but virtue that makes the difference. —*Voltaire*

**VIRTUE IS ITS OWN
REWARD.** There's a pleasure
in doing good which sufficiently
pays itself. —*Sir John Vanbrugh*

ONLY A VIRTUOUS PEOPLE

are capable of freedom.

As nations become more

corrupt and vicious,

they have more need of

masters. —*Benjamin Franklin*

★ ★ ★

WITHOUT VIRTUE,

happiness cannot be.

—*Thomas Jefferson*

VIRTUE, MORALITY, AND RELIGION. THIS IS THE ARMOR, MY FRIEND, AND THIS ALONE THAT RENDERS US INVINCIBLE. THESE ARE THE TACTICS WE SHOULD STUDY. IF WE LOSE THESE, WE ARE CONQUERED, FALLEN INDEED . . . SO LONG AS OUR MANNERS AND PRINCIPLES REMAIN SOUND, THERE IS NO DANGER. —*Patrick Henry*

Liberty can no more exist without

virtue and *independence*

than the body can live and move

without a soul. —*John Adams*

★ ★ ★

Fruits are

always of the same nature with the seeds and roots from which they come, and trees are known by the fruits they bear: as a man begets a man, and a beast a beast, that society of men which constitutes a government upon the foundation of justice, virtue, and the common good, will always have men to promote those ends; and that which intends the advancement of one man's desire and vanity will abound in those that will foment them. —*Algernon Sidney*

Unless virtue

guide us our choice must be wrong. —*William Penn*

NOTHING MORE COMPLETELY baffles one who is full of tricks and duplicity than straightforward and simple integrity in another. —*Charles Caleb Colton*

★ ★ ★

FEW MEN have virtue to withstand the highest bidder.

—*George Washington*

★ ★ ★

Virtue is the strong
stem of man's nature
and music is the
BLOSSOMING OF VIRTUE.

—*Confucius*

Men acquire a particular quality BY CONSTANTLY ACTING A PARTICULAR WAY . . . YOU BECOME JUST BY PERFORMING JUST ACTIONS, TEMPERATE BY PERFORMING TEMPERATE ACTIONS, BRAVE BY PERFORMING BRAVE ACTIONS. —*Aristotle*

The first virtue is to restrain the tongue; he approaches nearest to the gods who knows how to be silent, even though he is in the right. —*Cato the Younger*

EXEMPLIFY in your lives four tested, specific virtues: an attitude of gratitude, a longing for learning, a devotion to discipline, and a willingness to work. —*Thomas S. Monson*

What is virtue?

It is to hold yourself to your fullest development as a person and as a responsible member of the human community. —*Arthur Dobrin*

THERE IS VIRTUE in
country houses, in gardens and
orchards, in fields, streams and groves,
in rustic recreations and plain manners,
that neither cities nor universities
enjoy. —*Amos Bronson Alcott*

★ ★ ★

Sanity may be madness

BUT THE MADDEST OF ALL

is to see life as it is and

NOT AS IT SHOULD BE.

—*Don Quixote*

THERE IS THE TRUE JOY OF LIFE; TO
BE USED BY A PURPOSE RECOGNIZED
BY YOURSELF AS A MIGHTY ONE; TO
BE THOROUGHLY WORN OUT BEFORE
BEING THROWN ON THE SCRAP HEAP;
TO BE A FORCE OF NATURE INSTEAD
OF A FEVERISH, SELFISH LITTLE
CLOD OF AILMENTS AND GRIEVANCES
COMPLAINING THAT LIFE WILL NOT
DEVOTE ITSELF TO MAKING YOU
HAPPY. —*George Bernard Shaw*

★ ★ ★

The more VIRTUOUS ANY

MAN IS, the less easily

does he suspect others

to be vicious. —*Cicero*

He that has *energy enough to root out a vice,* should go further, and try to plant a virtue in its place, otherwise he will have his labor to renew. A strong soil that has produced weeds may be made to produce wheat. —*Charles Caleb Colton*

★ ★ ★

YOU HAVE TO CHOOSE
the best, every day,
without compromise
. . . guided by your
own virtue and highest
ambition. —*Philippa Gregory*

The door to

virtue

is heavy and hard to
push. —*Chinese Proverb*

Nine requisites for contented living: Health enough to make work a pleasure. Wealth enough to support your needs. Strength to battle with difficulties and overcome them. Grace enough to confess your sins and forsake them. Patience enough to toil until some good is accomplished. Charity enough to see some good in your neighbor. Love enough to move you to be useful and helpful to others. Faith enough to make real the things of God. Hope enough to remove all anxious fears concerning the future.

—*Johann Wolfgang von Goethe*

★ ★ ★

MY STRENGTH is

the strength of ten

because my heart is

pure. —*Lord Alfred Tennyson*

You will never have a greater or lesser dominion than that over yourself. **THE HEIGHT OF A MAN'S SUCCESS IS GAUGED BY HIS SELF-MASTERY;** the depth of his failure by his self-abandonment. And this law is the expansion of eternal justice. He who cannot establish dominion over himself will have no dominion over others. —*Leonardo da Vinci*

THERE NEVER WAS YET a truly great man THAT WAS NOT AT THE SAME TIME TRULY VIRTUOUS. —*Benjamin Franklin*